HELGE
RUBINSTEIN

CHOCOLATE PARFAIT

PENGUIN BOOKS

PENGUIN BOOKS

Published by the Penguin Group. Penguin Books Ltd, 27 Wrights Lane, London
w8 5TZ, England. Penguin Books USA Inc., 375 Hudson Street, New York,
New York 10014, USA. Penguin Books Australia Ltd, Ringwood, Victoria, Australia.
Penguin Books Canada Ltd, 10 Alcorn Avenue, Toronto, Ontario, Canada M4V 3B2.
Penguin Books (NZ) Ltd, 182–190 Wairau Road, Auckland 10, New Zealand · Penguin
Books Ltd, Registered Offices: Harmondsworth, Middlesex, England · These
recipes are from *The Chocolate Book*, by Helge Rubinstein, first published by Mac-
donald & Co (Publishers) 1981. Published in Penguin Books 1982. This edition
published 1996 · Copyright © Hilary Rubinstein Books Ltd, 1982. All rights reserved ·
Typeset by Rowland Phototypesetting Ltd, Bury St Edmunds, Suffolk. Printed in
England by Clays Ltd, St Ives plc · Except in the United States of America, this
book is sold subject to the condition that it shall not, by way of trade or otherwise,
be lent, re-sold, hired out, or otherwise circulated without the publisher's prior
consent in any form of binding or cover other than that in which it is published and
without a similar condition including this condition being imposed on the subsequent
purchaser · 10 9 8 7 6 5 4 3

CONTENTS

SIMPLE CHOCOLATE SOUFFLÉ

25 g (1 oz) cornflour
250 ml (scant ½ pint) milk
100 g (3½ oz) plain or bitter chocolate
2 teaspoons instant coffee powder (optional)
50 g (2 oz) sugar
3 egg yolks
5 egg whites
pinch of salt
1 tablespoon caster sugar
1 tablespoon icing sugar, sifted
butter and extra caster sugar to prepare soufflé dish

Prepare a 1-litre (2-pint) soufflé dish by buttering generously inside and sprinkling with caster sugar, and set the oven at gas mark 5 (190°C) 375°F.

Mix the cornflour to a smooth thin paste with a little of the milk. Put remaining milk into a heavy saucepan, add the chocolate, the coffee dissolved in a few drops of boiling water, and the sugar, and stir over a gentle heat until the chocolate has completely melted and the sugar has dissolved.

Pour in the cornflour paste in a thin stream, stirring constantly, then bring the mixture to the boil and boil for

1 minute, still stirring continuously. Remove from the heat.

Beat in the egg yolks one by one. Leave to cool a little.

The soufflé can be prepared ahead of time up to this point, but should, if necessary, be warmed a little before the next stage.

Whisk the whites with the pinch of salt until they begin to stand in soft peaks, then gradually beat in the caster sugar and continue to beat until they stand in stiff peaks but are not dry.

Now stir one third of the whites into the chocolate mixture until well blended, then fold the mixture gently but thoroughly into the remaining whites.

Pour immediately into the prepared soufflé dish and cook in the centre of the oven for 40 minutes.

Pull the soufflé gently to the front of the oven, sprinkle with a little of the sifted icing sugar and close the oven door again. After a few minutes, the icing sugar should have melted. Sprinkle with a little more, and repeat another two or three times until all the icing sugar has been used. This will give the soufflé an attractive glaze.

Serve immediately.

CHOCOLATE PANCAKES

You can make these as simple or as sophisticated as you like, to suit your public.

For the filling

100 g (3½ oz) chocolate
100 g (3½ oz) unsalted butter
25 g (1 oz) icing sugar or a little more, according to taste
1 tablespoon rum or brandy (optional)
50 g (2 oz) finely ground hazelnuts or praline (optional)

For the pancakes

125 g (4 oz) flour
pinch of salt
1 tablespoon icing sugar
2 eggs
300 ml (½ pint) milk
1 tablespoon brandy or water
25 g (1 oz) butter, melted
butter for frying
icing sugar

the filling first. Melt the chocolate (in a bowl over a pan of boiling water) and leave to cool a little.

Beat the butter with the icing sugar until light and fluffy, then beat in the chocolate, the rum or brandy and the nuts or praline. Taste for sweetness and leave in the refrigerator to harden.

To make the pancakes: sift the flour, salt and icing sugar into a bowl. Make a well in the centre and break in the eggs. Work the flour into the eggs and gradually add the milk until you have a smooth, light batter. Beat in the brandy or water and the melted butter. The batter should have the consistency of single cream. Let the batter rest a while if possible.

Heat a heavy frying or pancake pan, about 20 cm (8 in) diameter, add a knob of butter and as soon as it begins to foam, pour in a small ladleful of the batter. Turn the pan to cover the bottom completely, then pour back any excess batter as the pancakes should be as thin as possible. Cook the pancake on both sides, and set aside to keep warm. Repeat with remaining batter.

When ready to serve, place some chocolate filling down the centre of each pancake, roll it up and place on a heated serving dish. Reheat briefly under the grill if necessary.

Dredge with icing sugar before serving.

DEATH BY CHOCOLATE

There is a cautionary tale about a courtier of Louis XIII who was much devoted to the cause of improving the quality of chocolate. However, when he besmirched the honour of a lady of noble birth at the court, she invited him to drink a cup of chocolate, into which she had secretly slipped a deadly poison. Her suitor drained the cup, then drawing her to him just before he died, he whispered: 'the chocolate would have been better if you had added a little more sugar; the poison gives it a bitter flavour. Think of this the next time you offer a gentleman chocolate.'

Rumour had it that Charles II, who died in 1685, did not die of natural causes, but that his end had been brought about by his mistress, the Duchess of Portsmouth, who had offered him a cup of poisoned chocolate.

And suicide by chocolate?

> Jacob, with pistol in his hand,
> exclaims, 'Susannah, dear,
> without your love I'll kill myself?'
> Susannah quakes in fear.
> He lays the pistol to his head,
> Susannah pleads, 'Wait, wait!'
> 'Don't fret!' says Jacob, 'for this gun
> is only chocolate!'
>
> *Swiss poem, 1840*

SIMPLE CHOCOLATE MOUSSE

This is child's play to make and it never fails. If it is to be made by – or for – children, it is perfectly delicious even without alcohol. If possible, make it a day ahead so that the mixture can settle and, if you are adding spirits or liqueur, the flavour has time to mature.

> *175 g (6 oz) plain or bitter chocolate*
> *2 tablespoons brandy, rum, grand marnier, crème*
>   *de cacao, tia maria, chocolate peppermint liqueur*
>   *or water*
> *6 eggs*

Melt the chocolate with whatever liquid you are using (in a bowl over a pan of boiling water). Stir until smooth.

Separate the eggs and add the yolks one by one, beating in each one with a wooden spoon until well amalgamated before adding the next. The mixture will 'seize' and stiffen at first, but will gradually become soft, smooth and glossy.

Whip the egg whites until they stand in stiff peaks but are not completely dry.

Stir one third into the chocolate mixture until it is perfectly blended in, then lightly fold in the remaining whites with a spatula or spoon. Work as lightly as possible but take care that no white specks remain.

Pour into a glass or soufflé dish and refrigerate.

VARIATION: For an even smoother, richer, really velvety mousse, substitute 300 ml (½ pint) whipping cream, stiffly whipped, for the egg whites.

WHITE CHOCOLATE MOUSSE

Quick and simple, and refreshingly light, this must be whipped with a balloon whisk, by hand or with a powerful electric beater, in order to reach the necessary density. Make just before serving the meal and do not keep for more than about 1 hour.

> *100 g (3½ oz) plain or bitter chocolate*
> *4 egg whites*
> *4 tablespoons icing or caster sugar*

> For serving
> *1 tablespoon brandy or other liqueur (optional)*
> *single cream (optional)*

Grate the chocolate very finely.

Whip the egg whites until they stand in soft peaks, then whisk in the sugar until the mixture is very stiff and glossy. Fold in the grated chocolate.

Pour into individual bowls or serving glasses.

You can pour a little brandy, liqueur or cream round the edges just before serving.

NOTE: You can also blend a little powdered cinnamon with the caster sugar.

PETITS POTS AU CHOCOLAT

Individual chocolate creams

One of the simplest of the chocolate desserts, especially if you have an electric blender.

> *200 g (7 oz) plain or bitter chocolate*
> *300 ml (½ pint) single cream*
> *dash of salt*
> *3–4 drops vanilla essence*
> *1 egg*

If using a blender, break the chocolate into the blender jar.

Scald the cream and, when just boiling, pour on to the chocolate and blend till smooth. Blend in the salt and vanilla and the whole egg.

If you do not have a blender, scald the cream, take it off the heat and add the chocolate. Leave for 5 minutes for the chocolate to melt, then stir till smooth. Add the salt, the vanilla and the egg lightly beaten with a fork to amalgamate. Beat over a very gentle heat with a wooden spoon until absolutely smooth.

Pour into four to six individual pots or ramekin dishes and chill for at least 3–4 hours before serving. This mixture will set to a thick, smooth cream.

KENTUCKY CHOCOLATE PIE

Rich and fudgy, but to make it even fudgier, use soft brown sugar.

225 g (8 oz) shortcrust pastry
300 ml (½ pint) single cream
50 g (2 oz) plain or bitter chocolate
225 g (8 oz) sugar
2 tablespoons cornflour
2 tablespoons water
2 eggs
½ teaspoon vanilla essence
1 tablespoon rum
50 g (2 oz) butter, cut in small pieces

For decoration (optional)

150 ml (¼ pint) whipping cream
chocolate flakes (shaved off a chocolate bar with a
*   sharp knife or potato peeler)*

Set the oven at gas mark 6 (200°C) 400°F.
    Line a 23 cm (9 in) diameter flan case with the pastry,   9

prick it all over with a fork and bake blind for 20–25 minutes, until it is crisp and light golden brown. Leave to cool.

Put the cream, the chocolate and the sugar in a heavy saucepan and stir over a low heat until the chocolate and sugar have melted.

Stir the cornflour and water together to make a smooth paste.

Beat the eggs together lightly.

Add the cornflour mixture and the eggs to the saucepan, and stir continually over low heat for about 10 minutes. On no account allow the mixture to boil, but it should become very thick and smooth and, when ready, it should not taste in the least floury.

Remove from the heat, stir in the vanilla essence and the rum and beat in the butter.

Pour into the baked pastry shell and leave to chill.

Decorate with whipped cream and chocolate flakes if you like before serving.

CHOCOLATE CHIFFON PIE

Lighter than the Kentucky Chocolate Pie and very velvety.

> 225 g (8 oz) shortcrust pastry
> 10 g (scant ½ oz) gelatine
> 2 tablespoons water

300 ml (½ pint) milk
85 g (3 oz) plain or bitter chocolate
3 eggs
100 g (4 oz) sugar
½ teaspoon vanilla essence
pinch of salt
150 ml (¼ pint) whipping cream (optional)

Set the oven at gas mark 6 (200°C) 400°F.

Line a 23 cm (9 in) diameter flan case with the pastry, prick it all over with a fork and bake blind for 20–25 minutes until it is crisp and light golden brown. Leave to cool.

Sprinkle the gelatine into the water and leave to soften.

Heat the milk in a small, heavy saucepan, add the chocolate and stir until the chocolate has dissolved. Bring to just below boiling point.

Separate the eggs and beat the yolks lightly with all but 2 tablespoons of the sugar, then blend in a little of the hot chocolate milk. Return to the milk in the saucepan, add the vanilla and stir over a low heat until the custard begins to thicken. Do not allow to boil.

Remove from the heat, add the gelatine and stir until it has completely dissolved. Leave to cool.

When the mixture has cooled and begins to set, whip the egg whites with the pinch of salt until they stand in soft peaks. Add remaining sugar and beat until they are stiff. 11

Fold into the chocolate custard. Pour into the pastry case and chill until set.

Decorate with whipped cream if you like before serving.

VARIATION: To make CHOCOLATE RUM CHIFFON PIE, make the custard without adding the chocolate to the milk.

After stirring in the gelatine, divide the custard in half and add 50 g (2 oz) chocolate, broken into small pieces, to one half, stirring until it has melted and the custard is quite smooth.

Add 1 tablespoon rum to the other half of the custard.

Fold half the whipped egg whites into each custard when cooled, then pour the chocolate mixture first into the pastry case. Smooth over the top and pour over the rum mixture evenly to cover.

They will set in two distinct layers, so that the chocolate comes as a surprise when you cut the pie, and the rum adds an extra kick.

For a marbled effect, let the two custards nearly set, then pour into the pastry shell in alternate strips. Swirl together with a two-pronged fork or spatula.

CHOCOLATE YOGURT AMBROSIA

Refreshing and very quick and simple to make.

300 ml (½ pint) plain yogurt
300 ml (½ pint) double cream
25 g (1 oz) plain or bitter chocolate
6–8 teaspoons soft brown sugar (or more)

Whip the yogurt and cream together until the mixture becomes light and quite thick.

Grate the chocolate finely and blend in.

Pour into six or eight individual ramekin dishes and sprinkle each dish with a teaspoon of soft brown sugar.

Refrigerate for several hours or overnight. The mixture will have set like a junket, and the sugar will have dissolved into a rich brown syrup.

Sprinkle on a little more sugar before serving, if you wish.

· ·

'When you have breakfasted well and fully, if you will drink a big cup of chocolate at the end you will have digested the whole perfectly three hours later, and you will still be able to dine.'

J.-A. BRILLAT-SAVARIN, *Physiologie du goût*, 1825

· ·

CREAM CHEESE AND COCOA

The Italians have a marvellously simple dessert called *ricotta al caffè* which consists of mounds of ricotta or curd cheese, some freshly ground coffee, sugar and rum or brandy. It is just as good with cocoa instead of coffee, but the cocoa should be a really good quality, 'pure' cocoa to get the delicately bitter flavour.

The ricotta must be very fresh and moist – if not, it is better to use curd cheese.

This dessert is deceptively rich, and though these quantities may not seem very great, they should be ample for four.

> *250 g (8 oz) ricotta or curd cheese (see above)*
> *4 tablespoons 'pure' cocoa powder*
> *4 dessertspoons sugar*
> *4 dessertspoons rum or brandy*

Pass the ricotta or curd cheese through a nylon sieve or whisk it briefly to make it smooth, then put a mound on each plate.

Add a little heap of cocoa and one of sugar separately on the plates, and dribble the rum or brandy over the cheese.

Everyone then dips each spoonful of cheese first into the cocoa and then into the sugar.

CHOCOLATE REFRIGERATOR CAKE

Refrigerator cakes are quick and easy to make and require no cooking. They freeze extremely well and are a useful standby.

While this will never be exactly a plain dessert, you can make it more or less luxurious, according to whether you use digestive or tea biscuits, sponge fingers, or – the ultimate luxury – some good, hard Italian macaroons. The brandy is of course optional, although I would hate to leave it out. The milk is only necessary with sponge fingers, which otherwise remain too dry.

> *250 g (8 oz) plain or bitter chocolate*
> *3 tablespoons very strong black coffee*
> *250 g (8 oz) unsalted butter*
> *200 g (6 oz) sugar*
> *1 tablespoon cocoa*
> *3 eggs*
> *approx. 250 g (8 oz) biscuits (see above)*
> *2–3 tablespoons brandy (optional)*
> *2–3 tablespoons milk (optional) see above*

Melt the chocolate with the coffee (in a bowl over a pan of boiling water) and leave to cool.

Whisk the butter with the sugar until light and fluffy, then whisk in the cocoa. Separate the eggs and beat in the yolks one by one.

Blend the melted chocolate into the mixture.

Whisk the whites until they stand in stiff peaks and fold gently but thoroughly into the chocolate cream.

Line a 23–25 cm (9–10 in) diameter loose-bottomed cake tin with foil. If you are using digestive or tea biscuits, break them up roughly and make a first layer on the bottom of the tin. If you are using macaroons, lay them in a single layer on the bottom. Dribble on a little of the brandy.

If you are using sponge fingers, blend the milk and the brandy in a saucer and briefly dip in each finger before using them to line the bottom of the tin.

Spread a thick layer of the chocolate cream over the biscuits, and then repeat until everything has been used up.

Refrigerate overnight, or freeze for about 2 hours before turning out and serving.

NOTE: To make it even richer, fold 50 g (2 oz) chopped walnuts and/or 50 g (2 oz) chopped glacé cherries into the chocolate cream.

ECONOMICAL CHOCOLATE ICE CREAM

This is the least rich of the ice creams, but it has a good chocolaty taste, a smooth texture and dark colour. Serve plain or with whipped cream, or sprinkled with chopped nuts or praline. This is also the best ice to use with mer-

ingues or in such dishes as *bombes*, Baked Alaska or Chocolat
Liégeois.

To give added depth of flavour, also try making this ice
with brown sugar.

> *300 ml (½ pint) milk*
> *125 g (4 oz) plain or bitter chocolate*
> *3 egg yolks*
> *50 g (2 oz) sugar*

Scald the milk, then remove from the heat and add the
chocolate. Leave to melt and then stir until smooth.

Meanwhile whisk the yolks with the sugar until pale and
thick, then slowly whisk in the chocolate milk.

Return to the saucepan and stir over a gentle heat until
the mixture thickens.

Pour into a freezing tray or serving dish and freeze.

Remove from the freezer 1 hour before serving and store
in the refrigerator.

RICH CHOCOLATE ICE CREAM

This is a good creamy ice, smooth and rich but not cloying,
and you can vary the amount of whipped cream you add to
suit your taste. This ice is particularly good sprinkled with
a thick layer of chopped hazelnuts or toasted almonds before
serving.

300 ml (½ pint) single cream or milk
125 g (4 oz) plain or bitter chocolate
2 teaspoons instant coffee powder (optional)
4 egg yolks
100–125 g (3–4 oz) sugar
150–300 ml (¼–½ pint) whipping or double cream
    (see above)

Scald the single cream or milk, then remove from the heat and add the chocolate and coffee. Leave to melt, then stir until smooth.

Whisk the yolks with the sugar until pale and thick, then slowly whisk in the chocolate milk.

Return to the saucepan and stir over a gentle heat until the mixture thickens. Remove from the heat and leave to cool.

Whip the cream until thick but light and fold into the cooled custard.

Pour into a freezing tray or serving dish and freeze.

Remove from the freezer half an hour before serving and keep in the refrigerator.

VARIATION: To make CHOCOLATE PRALINE ICE CREAM use a little less sugar and stir in 125–175 g (4–6 oz) praline before folding in the whipping cream.

CHOCOLATE HONEYCOMB ICE

Very light, with an interesting honeycomb texture; children love this ice.

> *300 ml (½ pint) single cream or milk, or a blend of*
> *   the two*
> *125 g (4 oz) plain or bitter chocolate*
> *4 egg yolks*
> *75 g (3 oz) sugar*
> *150 ml (¼ pint) double cream*
> *2 egg whites*

Scald the cream or milk, then remove from the heat and add the chocolate. Leave to melt, then stir until smooth.

Meanwhile separate the eggs and whisk the yolks with the sugar until they are pale and thick, then slowly whisk in the chocolate milk.

Return to the saucepan and stir over a gentle heat until the mixture thickens. Remove from the heat and leave to cool.

Whip the cream until light and then fold in the cooled custard.

Whisk the whites until they stand in firm peaks and fold into the mixture.

Pour into a serving dish and freeze. The mixture will slightly separate and the frozen ice will have a dense texture at the bottom, and a lighter, 'honeycomb' texture on top.

Remove from the freezer half an hour before serving and leave in the refrigerator.

CHOCOLATE, MOCHA AND MARSHMALLOW ICE CREAM

1 (140 g, 5 oz) packet marshmallows
225 g (8 oz) plain or bitter chocolate
4 tablespoons very strong coffee
4 egg yolks
300 ml (½ pint) double cream

Melt the marshmallows, chocolate and coffee together in a basin over a pan of simmering water.

Beat the yolks until pale and fluffy, then add to the chocolate mixture slowly, stirring well. Continue to cook over simmering water until the mixture thickens slightly. Remove from the heat and leave to cool.

Whip the cream lightly and fold in. Pour into a serving dish and freeze.

NOTE: You can also keep aside a little of the chocolate, grate it coarsely, and stir it into the cooled mixture when you fold in the whipped cream.

CHOCOLATE PARFAIT

Velvety smooth, richly chocolaty but refreshing, this really perfect dessert is quick and easy to make provided you have a powerful electric mixer. Use unsweetened chocolate if possible; if not, be sure to add the coffee to counteract the extra sweetness, as the frozen consistency would not be as good if you used less sugar.

> 125 g (4 oz) sugar
> 150 ml (¼ pint) water
> 125 g (4 oz) unsweetened or bitter chocolate
> 4 egg yolks
> 1 tablespoon brandy (optional)
> 1 tablespoon very strong black coffee (optional) see
>   above
> 300 ml (½ pint) whipping cream

Bring the sugar and water to the boil in a heavy saucepan, stirring until the sugar has dissolved. Boil briskly for 3 minutes. Then remove from the heat and add the chocolate, stirring until the chocolate has melted and the syrup is smooth.

Meanwhile whisk the yolks until they are pale. Slowly pour in the hot chocolate syrup and continue to whisk until the mixture has cooled. Add the brandy and coffee.

Whip the cream until light and bulky but not stiff, and fold into the cooled chocolate cream.

Pour into individual parfait glasses or ramekin dishes and freeze.

Serve straight from the freezer.

CHOCOLATE SAUCES

There are those for whom no ice cream is complete without its chocolate sauce, preferably poured over while hot, thickly congealing as it meets, and melts, the ice cream.

Quick Chocolate Sauce

Economical and very good hot or cold. It thickens as it cools.

> *175 g (6 oz) sugar*
> *300 ml (½ pint) water*
> *50 g (2 oz) cocoa powder*
> *pinch of ground cinnamon*

Put all the ingredients into a saucepan and stir over low heat until the sugar has completely dissolved and the sauce is smooth. Bring quickly to the boil and boil for 1 minute.

Rich Chocolate Sauce

225 g (8 oz) plain or bitter chocolate
1 tablespoon very strong black coffee
1 tablespoon brandy
300 ml (½ pint) double or single cream

Put all the ingredients into a saucepan and stir over a moderate heat until the chocolate has melted and the sauce is smooth. Serve hot or cold.

Bittersweet Chocolate Sauce

125 g (4 oz) plain or bitter chocolate
175 g (6 oz) sugar
300 ml (½ pint) single or double cream
1 tablespoon strong black coffee
1 tablespoon rum or brandy (optional)

Put the chocolate and sugar into the top of a double boiler, or into a very heavy saucepan, and stir over gentle heat until the chocolate has melted. Cover and simmer for 20 minutes (do not allow to burn) – this gives the sauce its distinctive slightly bitter taste.

Take off the heat, stir in the cream and other ingredients and stir until smooth.

Serve hot or cold.

Hot Chocolate Fudge Sauce

150 ml (¼ pint) double cream
50 g (2 oz) butter
50 g (2 oz) soft dark brown sugar
50 g (2 oz) light brown sugar
25 g (1 oz) cocoa powder
pinch of salt

Heat the cream with the butter and stir until smooth. Add both the sugars and stir over moderate heat until the sugar has dissolved and the sauce is quite smooth.

Add the cocoa and salt, stir until smooth, bring just to the boil and serve very hot.

QUICK CHOCOLATE CAKE

Almost instant, economical and very basic, this is one of those 'never fail' family recipes that everyone should have in their repertoire. To be truly quick, you need an electric mixer, and should use a soft margarine.

125 g (4 oz) self-raising flour
1 teaspoon baking powder
125 g (4 oz) caster sugar
125 g (4 oz) soft margarine

2 large or 3 small eggs
25 g (1 oz) cocoa powder
1 teaspoon instant coffee powder
3 tablespoons very hot water

For the icing

100 g (4 oz) icing sugar
25 g (1 oz) cocoa powder
50 g (2 oz) butter
3 tablespoons water
75 g (3 oz) sugar

Set the oven at gas mark 4 (180°C) 350°F.

Sift the flour and baking powder into a large mixing bowl, add sugar, margarine and eggs. Mix the cocoa and coffee powder to a smooth paste with warm water just off the boil and add to the bowl.

Starting on the lowest speed, begin to mix the ingredients, and as soon as they begin to blend increase the speed and beat at top speed for one minute only.

Divide the mixture between two buttered or non-stick 18 or 20 cm (7–8 in) diameter sandwich tins, spreading the mixture evenly and smoothing the top, and bake for 25–30 minutes, until the tops of the cakes are firm. Turn out on to wire trays and leave to cool.

Sift the icing sugar and cocoa into a bowl.

Put the remaining ingredients into a small saucepan and

heat gently, stirring till the sugar is dissolved. Bring to the boil and immediately pour into the bowl, stirring to a smooth, thin cream.

Leave to cool until the cake is ready to be iced: the mixture will thicken as it cools.

When the cake has cooled, use half the mixture to sandwich the two cakes together and spread remaining icing over the top.

. . . .

Katharine Hepburn, seventy, actress, asked how she stays trim: 'I don't have to watch my figure as I never had much of one to watch. What you see before you is the result of a lifetime of chocolate.'

Time Magazine, 17 November 1980

. . . .

MARBLE CAKE

An old-time children's favourite.

175 g (6 oz) butter or margarine
175 g (6 oz) sugar
3 large eggs
175 g (6 oz) plain flour
1 teaspoon baking powder
grated rind of ½ lemon

1 tablespoon cocoa powder
1 tablespoon icing sugar

Set the oven at gas mark 4 (180°C) 350°F.

Generously butter a 20 cm (8 in) diameter kugelhopf tin or use a springform baking tin with the central funnel, and sprinkle with fine breadcrumbs or ground almonds.

Cream the butter or margarine with the sugar until very light and fluffy, then add the eggs one by one and continue to beat until the mixture is very light.

Sift the flour with the baking powder and fold in.

Divide the mixture into almost equal halves and add the grated lemon rind to the larger 'half'.

Blend the cocoa thoroughly into the remaining part of the mixture.

Spoon half the white mixture into the bottom of the cake tin. Top with half the chocolate mixture and repeat. The layers will be uneven, and give a 'marbled' effect after baking. Smooth over the top and bake for 50 minutes to 1 hour, or until a skewer inserted into the centre of the cake comes out clean.

Leave to cool a little, then turn out of the tin on to a wire baking tray, and when almost cooled, sprinkle the top with the sifted icing sugar.

RICH CHOCOLATE CAKE

This is a really rich, dark cake – the kind indulgent mothers might put into a school tuck box as it keeps moist for a long time.

225 g (8 oz) butter or margarine
225 g (8 oz) sugar
1 tablespoon very strong black coffee
1 tablespoon sherry
4 eggs
100 g (3½ oz) cocoa powder
225 g (8 oz) self-raising flour
125 g (4 oz) ground almonds

For the butter icing

100 g (3½ oz) plain or bitter chocolate
1 tablespoon very strong black coffee
75 g (3 oz) unsalted butter
150 g (5 oz) icing sugar
1 tablespoon sherry (optional)

For the glacé icing

100 g (3½ oz) plain or bitter chocolate
2 tablespoons water
75 g (3 oz) icing sugar
15 g (½ oz) butter

Set the oven at gas mark 4 (180°C) 350°F.

Cream the butter or margarine and sugar together until white and very fluffy.

Beat in the coffee and sherry.

Beat the eggs together lightly with a fork.

Sift the cocoa and flour together, and blend in the ground almonds.

Alternately beat the eggs and the dry ingredients into the butter mixture.

Pour into a well-greased 25 cm (10 in) diameter baking tin, preferably a springform tin, and bake for about 1 hour, or until the top has risen slightly and is firm to the touch, and a skewer inserted into the centre of the cake comes out clean.

Allow to cool for about 15 minutes, then remove from the tin and leave to cool thoroughly on a wire cake rack.

To make the butter icing, melt the chocolate with the coffee (in a bowl over a pan of boiling water). Stir until smooth and leave to cool a little.

Beat the butter and sugar together until very light and fluffy. Beat in the chocolate and the sherry.

When the cake is quite cold, split it across the centre and sandwich together with the butter icing.

Make the chocolate glacé icing by putting the chocolate into a small saucepan with the water. Stir over a low heat until the chocolate has melted and forms a smooth sauce. Add the icing sugar, stir until smooth, then raise the heat 29 and bring to the boil. Boil, stirring constantly, until a small amount of the mixture dropped into cold water forms a soft ball (116°C or 240°F on a sugar thermometer), and the mixture in the pan begins to throw thick bubbles. Remove from the heat, stir in the butter and pour quickly and evenly over the cake, smoothing any surplus that drips off round the sides of the cake.

Leave to set for at least 1 hour before serving.

TRUFFLE CAKE

A bitter-sweet, intensely chocolaty cake, with just a hint of orange, filled and covered with a rich truffle mixture – how much more satisfyingly chocolaty can you get?

For the cake

200 g (7 oz) plain or bitter chocolate
100 g (4 oz) unsalted butter
2 tablespoons caster sugar
4 eggs
75 g (3 oz) plain flour
½ teaspoon baking powder
icing sugar, for dusting (optional)

For the filling

225 g (8 oz) plain or bitter chocolate
225 g (8 oz) unsalted butter
225 g (8 oz) icing sugar
4 tablespoons orange juice
4 tablespoons orange curaçao

Set the oven at gas mark 4 (180°C) 350°F.

Melt the chocolate (in a bowl over a pan of boiling water), stir till smooth and leave to cool.

Beat the butter with 1 tablespoon of caster sugar until pale and fluffy. Separate the eggs and beat in the yolks one by one. Beat in the melted, cooled chocolate.

Sift the flour with the baking powder and fold into the mixture.

Beat the whites until they begin to stand in peaks, then beat in the remaining caster sugar. Fold the cake mixture gently but thoroughly into the meringue. Pour into a buttered 20 cm (8 in) diameter cake tin, preferably springform or loose-bottomed, and bake for 40–45 minutes, or until a skewer inserted just comes out clean. Remove from the oven, leave to cool a little, then turn out of the tin and leave to cool on a wire rack.

Prepare the filling as for making Quick Truffles, and beat in half the orange juice and liqueur.

When the cake is quite cold, slice it in half and lightly

dribble the remaining orange juice and liqueur over both halves.

Sandwich the cake together with half the truffle mixture and spread or pipe the remainder over the top.

Lightly dust with a little icing sugar before serving, if you wish.

CHOCOLATE SPONGE CAKE

Very light, and best eaten very fresh, sandwiched with vanilla-flavoured, lightly whipped cream. You can also flavour the cream with puréed, sieved raspberries, as these blend particularly well with chocolate.

3 large eggs
pinch of salt
125 g (4 oz) sugar
75 g (3 oz) plain flour
½ teaspoon baking powder
20 g (¾ oz) cocoa powder

For the filling
300 ml (½ pint) double or whipping cream
a few drops vanilla essence
icing sugar, for dredging

32   Set the oven at gas mark 6 (200°C) 400°F.

Separate the eggs and whisk the whites with the pinch of salt until they stand in peaks. Slowly whisk in the sugar. Beat the yolks together lightly with a fork and whisk them into the whites very slowly. In this way the mixture should remain very thick, light and bulky.

Sift the flour together with the baking powder and the cocoa, and fold lightly but thoroughly into the sponge mixture, using a tablespoon or a spatula.

Butter two 20 or 23 cm (8 or 9 in) diameter sandwich tins and dredge them lightly with flour. Divide the mixture evenly between the two tins, smooth over the tops and bake for 25 minutes, or until the tops have risen but are firm, and the cake has shrunk a little from the sides.

Leave to cool for 5 minutes, then turn out on to a wire cake rack.

Whip the cream lightly with the vanilla essence and a teaspoon of icing sugar, and sandwich the cakes together when cool. Dust the top with a little more icing sugar.

SACHERTORTE

The most famous of all the Viennese cakes, Sachertorte has been the subject of a great many myths, stories and arguments. This is how Joseph Wechsberg tells the tale in *The Cooking of Vienna's Empire* (Time-Life Books).

It is not true, as one legend has it, that the *Sachertorte* was invented by the notorious Frau Anna Sacher. This formidable, cigar-smoking owner of the Hotel Sacher irritated His Majesty, the ascetic Emperor Franz Joseph I, by encouraging the frivolous goings-on between the youthful archdukes and the lithe, lissom members of the Vienna Opera ballet. In fact, the *Sachertorte* had been invented in 1832 by the founder of the Sacher line, Franz, while he was serving as Prince Metternich's chef.

'He bothered me all the time to invent something new, as though my pastries were not good enough,' Franz Sacher said. 'So I just threw some ingredients together and that's it.' 'He' was Prince Metternich, and 'it' became the *Sachertorte*. Fortunately the Prince didn't demand that it be called *Metternichtorte*. He might have, if he had foreseen its world-wide success, but even a Metternich cannot foresee the future.

Since then there have been countless recipes for the 'Original' *Sachertorte*. It is the only *Torte* on earth that became the issue of a celebrated court case, which created more excitement in Vienna and consumed more newspaper space than a minor war. The issue was: who had the right to call his product the 'genuine' *Sachertorte* – the Hotel Sacher, which traded on the family connection with the *Sachertorte*'s creator, or Demel's, which had bought the right to fix the 'Genuine *Sachertorte*' seal (in the finest plain chocolate, of course) on its *Torten*? Demel's had acquired the right from Edouard Sacher, the grandson of creator Franz Sacher and the last scion of the dynasty. The recipe was published, with Edouard Sacher's permission, in *Die Wiener Konditorei*, by Hans Skrach. It starts out with 14 egg yolks, just to give you an idea of its scope.

The question kept the public and the courts of Vienna busy for seven long years. It is known in Vienna as the 'Sweet Seven Years' War'. Eventually, Austria's highest court decided that the Hotel Sacher had the right to make and sell the 'Genuine *Sachertorte*'. That was the end of the law-suit, but not of the popular argument. Demel's promptly announced they were going to sell the *Ur-Sachertorte*, the very first version. Since then a great many people, including some prominent members of the Sugar Bakers' Guild, have spoken out in favour of Demel's. Both Demel's and the Hotel Sacher send their *Sachertorten* in wooden boxes all over the world, and one can only say that both versions are light, delicate and distinctive.

Vienna's leading chefs are no help when it comes to defining the proper recipe for the *Sachertorte*. A former Demel's man puts the apricot jam inside, a method frowned upon by other experts.

While not pretending to be the 'genuine' Sachertorte, nor yet the 'Ur-Sachertorte', this recipe is as near to the Viennese taste as I can get. The cake should be very dark and chocolaty, but fairly dry, with a sweet, dark icing. I have given instructions for slicing the cake in half and sandwiching it with the apricot glaze, but those who prefer can halve the quantity of the glaze, and only brush the top thinly with it. The chocolate used should be as bitter as possible, and the bitter almond essence is an essential ingredient which makes all the difference to the final taste of the cake.

175 g (6 oz) bitter chocolate
125 g (4 oz) unsalted butter
125 g (4 oz) sugar

4 egg yolks
¼ teaspoon bitter almond essence
125 g (4 oz) plain flour
¼ teaspoon baking powder
5 egg whites
pinch of salt

For the glaze

2 tablespoons apricot jam
1 tablespoon water
good squeeze lemon juice

For the icing

75 g (3 oz) sugar
4 tablespoons water
100 g (3½ oz) bitter chocolate

Set the oven at gas mark 3 (160°C) 325°F.

Melt the chocolate (in a bowl over a pan of boiling water).

Cream the butter with the sugar until very light and fluffy, then add the egg yolks one by one and continue to beat until the mixture is light and smooth. Blend in the melted chocolate and the almond essence.

Sift the flour with the baking powder and then sift again into the mixing bowl. Fold the flour into the mixture, using a metal spoon or spatula, until thoroughly blended.

Whisk the egg whites with the salt until they are stiff but

not dry, and incorporate into the mixture, folding gently but thoroughly with a metal spoon or spatula, until no streaks of white remain.

Pour into a buttered and floured loose-bottomed 25 cm (10 in) diameter baking tin, and bake in the centre of the oven for 1 hour, or until the cake is firm to the touch and has shrunk slightly from the sides of the tin.

Leave to cool a little, then remove the cake from the tin and allow it to cool thoroughly on a wire rack before glazing and icing.

To make the glaze, heat the apricot jam with the water and lemon juice and bring briefly to the boil. If necessary, pass through a nylon strainer. Slice the cake in half and sandwich together with most of the glaze. Brush the remainder over the top of the cake so that it is only just moist. Leave to set.

To make the icing, bring the sugar and water to the boil, stirring all the time until the sugar has dissolved. Remove from the heat, add the chocolate and stir until the chocolate has completely melted and the mixture is quite smooth. Return to the heat and boil until a temperature of 116°C (240°F) has been reached on a sugar thermometer, or a small amount of the mixture dropped in cold water forms a soft ball.

Remove immediately from the heat, and continue to stir until the mixture ceases to bubble.

Pour quickly and evenly over the top of the cake, allowing 37 the icing to flow down the sides. Use a palette knife to smooth the icing round the sides of the cake but do not touch the top, or it will lose its sheen.

If you like you can keep back a small part of the icing, and when the icing on the cake has begun to set, warm the remainder slightly, adding a drop of water if necessary, and drip the famous Sacher signature over the top of the cake from the tip of a spoon or knife.

DEVIL'S FOOD CAKE

A really dark, rich and moist cake, with a thick fudgy icing.

125 g (4 oz) plain or bitter chocolate
150 ml (¼ pint) water
125 g (4 oz) butter
225 g (8 oz) soft brown sugar
2 eggs
225 g (8 oz) plain flour
½ teaspoon baking powder
pinch of salt
150 ml (¼ pint) soured cream

For the chocolate fudge icing

150 ml (¼ pint) single cream or milk
50 g (2 oz) plain or bitter chocolate
100 g (3½ oz) sugar

50 g (2 oz) butter
¼ teaspoon vanilla essence

Set the oven at gas mark 4 (180°C) 350°F.

Melt the chocolate with the water (in a bowl over a pan of boiling water). Stir until smooth and leave to cool.

Cream the butter and sugar together until light and fluffy. Add the eggs, one at a time, and beat until very light and smooth.

Blend in the melted chocolate.

Sift the flour with the baking powder and salt and beat into the mixture alternately with the soured cream. Pour into two buttered and floured 23 cm (9 in) diameter sponge tins and bake for 25–30 minutes. Leave to cool a little, then turn out on to a wire rack.

To make the icing, put the cream or milk into a small saucepan, break in the chocolate, add the sugar and melt over a moderate heat. When the chocolate and sugar have melted, bring to the boil, and boil, stirring well, until the mixture thickens and a small amount, dropped into cold water, forms a soft ball, or a sugar thermometer registers 116°C (240°F).

Remove from the heat, add the butter cut into pieces, and the vanilla, and stir until smooth. When the mixture has cooled a little, beat vigorously with a wooden spoon until it has thickened sufficiently to spread. Sandwich the two cakes together with half the icing, and spread remaining icing over the top.

CHOCOLATE MILLE FEUILLES

Very simple and quick to prepare with ready-made puff pastry.

> *225 g (8 oz) puff pastry*

For the filling

> *125 g (4 oz) plain or bitter chocolate*
> *2 tablespoons water*
> *1 tablespoon brandy*
> *300 ml (½ pint) double or whipping cream – or a*
>   *little less*

For the icing

> *squeeze lemon juice*
> *hot water*
> *2 tablespoons icing sugar*

Set the oven at gas mark 7 (220°C) 425°F.

Roll out the pastry into a rectangle ¼ cm (⅛ in) thick, then cut it into three equal rectangles. Lift each individual rectangle of pastry up and slap it down flat on the pastry board several times, then roll out again to the original thickness. This allows the pastry to shrink before, rather than during, the baking.

Place each sheet on to a dampened baking tray and bake in the centre of the oven for 15–20 minutes, or until well

40

risen and pale brown. Do not allow to get too dark, or it will taste bitter.

Leave to cool on wire baking trays.

Meanwhile prepare the filling. Melt the chocolate with the water and the brandy (in a bowl over a pan of boiling water). Stir until smooth and leave to cool.

Whip the cream till light and bulky.

Prepare the icing by stirring the lemon juice and enough hot water, a few drops at a time, into the icing sugar to make a smooth paste, just thick enough to spread easily.

When the pastry sheets have cooled, trim them if necessary to equal size and shape, and spread the icing over one sheet. Drizzle three thin parallel lines of the chocolate sauce down the length of the iced sheet, then draw the back of a knife across the lines to make the characteristic mille feuilles design.

Spread half the cream over one of the other sheets and drizzle on half the remaining chocolate sauce. Mingle it slightly into the cream with the knife. Place the second pastry layer on top and repeat. Top with the iced pastry sheet.

CHOCOLATE ROULADE

A really light dessert cake.

For the cake

6 eggs
200 g (7 oz) caster sugar
1 teaspoon vanilla sugar or a few drops vanilla
  essence
50 g (2 oz) cocoa powder

For the filling

125 g (4 oz) plain or bitter chocolate
2 tablespoons brandy or water
300 ml (½ pint) double or whipping cream

Set the oven at gas mark 4 (180°C) 350°F.

Separate the eggs and whisk the yolks with the sugar and vanilla until light and pale.

Sift the cocoa and fold it in lightly.

Whisk the whites until stiff but not dry and fold carefully into the mixture.

Pour into a buttered Swiss roll tin, approximately 33 × 20 cm (13 × 8 in) and spread evenly.

Bake for 20–25 minutes, until the top is springy to the touch. Do not overcook.

Remove from the oven and allow to cool for 10–15

minutes in the tin, then turn out carefully on to a sheet of greaseproof paper. Leave to cool and, when almost cold, roll up with the paper like a Swiss Roll.

To make the filling, melt the chocolate with the brandy or water (in a bowl over a pan of boiling water) and stir until smooth. Leave to cool a little, then open up the sponge roll and spread on the chocolate mixture.

Whip the cream lightly and spread thickly over the chocolate. Roll up again and place carefully on a serving dish or platter.

You can decorate the roulade with more whipped cream and chocolate flakes or curls (shaved off a chocolate bar with a sharp knife or potato peeler), finely chopped nuts or roasted almonds before serving if you wish.

ULTIMATE CHOCOLATE CAKE

The most densely chocolaty of them all, this is really a dessert gâteau, about which one correspondent rapturized 'you feel that your tongue has reached to the very soul of chocolate'.

Do not bother to make this unless you can use the very best quality bitter or semi-sweet dessert or cooking chocolate; if you cannot obtain unsweetened chocolate, use pure cocoa.

This cake will feed 4–6; double the quantities once you are confident and use a 25 cm (10 in) springform tin.

Delicious- I can taste the guilt...

calman

250 g (9 oz) bitter or cooking chocolate (see page 43)
25 g (1 oz) unsweetened chocolate or cocoa powder
   (see page 43)
2 heaped teaspoons instant coffee powder
2 tablespoons rum
50 g (2 oz) icing sugar
1 dessertspoon cornflour
3 large or 4 medium eggs
a few drops vanilla essence
150 ml (¼ pint) double cream

For serving (optional)

150 ml (¼ pint) whipping cream
a few drops vanilla essence

Heat the oven to gas mark 4 (180°C) 350°F.

Prepare a 23 cm (9 in) diameter, 5 cm (2 in) deep sponge
or flan tin by buttering and flouring it liberally, then line
with a few strips of butter paper.

Melt both chocolates together with the coffee dissolved
in 2 tablespoons hot water and the rum (in a bowl over a
pan of boiling water). Stir till smooth and leave to cool.

Blend the cornflour into the icing sugar together with
cocoa if you are using it, and sift together twice.

Beat the eggs together lightly with the vanilla essence,
thoroughly blend in the icing sugar mixture and whisk with
a balloon whisk, preferably with an electric beater, until   45

they are very thick and foamy, and have at least trebled in volume.

Blend in the cooled chocolate mixture.

Whip the cream lightly and fold in carefully.

Pour into the prepared tin and bake in the centre of the oven for about one hour, or until a skewer inserted comes out clean. Turn off the oven, leave the door open and leave to cool. The cake will sink as it cools. Turn out of the tin and serve, if you like, with the lightly whipped, vanilla flavoured cream.

BROWNIES

Brownies are an American classic – as corny as blueberry pie. Everyone has their own favourite recipe, and the controversy has even reached the pages of *Private Eye*, where a correspondent writes that 'brownies should be fudgy and nutty and disgustingly yummy'. On that at least everyone can agree and there is also a general consensus that true brownies can only be made with unsweetened cooking chocolate. What better recipe to give then, than the one put out by the makers of Baker's Cooking Chocolate themselves, for though I have tried many different recipes, and found them all delicious, this is certainly one of the best.

110 g (4 oz) unsweetened cooking chocolate
50 g (2 oz) unsalted butter
75 g (3 oz) plain flour
good pinch baking powder
good pinch salt
2 eggs
175 g (6 oz) sugar
1 teaspoon vanilla essence
50 g (2 oz) pecans or walnuts

Set the oven at gas mark 4 (180°C) 350°F.

Melt the chocolate (in a bowl over a pan of boiling water) and, when cooled a little, add the butter cut into small pieces. Stir until the butter has melted and blended with the chocolate.

Sift the flour with the baking powder and salt.

Beat the eggs together with the sugar and vanilla until fluffy and blend in the chocolate and butter mixture.

Fold in the flour and then the roughly chopped nuts.

Pour into a greased 20 cm (8 in) square baking tin and bake for 20–25 minutes, or until a skewer inserted just comes out clean.

Allow to cool, then cut into squares – they will turn fudgy as they cool.

VARIATION: MARBLED BROWNIES Use 50 g (2 oz) chocolate only; melt and set aside. Melt butter separately.

Proceed as above until flour and nuts have been folded into butter and eggs. Divide mixture in half, add chocolate to one half. Pour first chocolate, then white mixture into baking tin, draw a knife through to 'marble' them, and bake as above.

. . . .

The chocolate bar is an edible American flag, a security blanket for the distraught, a barometer of a nation's economic health.

The New York Times, Sunday, 25 February 1979

. . . .

CHOCOLATE COOKIES

125 g (4 oz) plain or bitter chocolate
125 g (4 oz) butter
1 egg
175 g (6 oz) granulated or soft brown sugar
175 g (6 oz) self-raising flour

Set the oven at gas mark 6 (200°C) 400°F.

Melt the chocolate (in a bowl over a pan of boiling water), leave to cool a little, then add the butter cut into pieces and stir until smooth.

Break the egg into a bowl. Add the sugar and stir in with a fork. Blend in the melted chocolate and butter mixture and then work in the sifted flour to make a stiff dough.

Roll the dough into balls each the size of a large walnut and place, well spaced, on a buttered or non-stick baking sheet.

Bake for 10–12 minutes, until they have spread out into round cookies, and the top of each is cracked like parched earth.

Remove from the oven and leave to cool and crisp on a wire tray.

CHOCOLATE CHIP COOKIES

Another American classic, much cheaper and infinitely more 'moreish' when made at home. It is easiest to use ready-made chocolate chips, but a good plain eating chocolate cut into small chips will also do.

125 g (4 oz) butter
50 g (2 oz) soft light brown sugar
50 g (2 oz) granulated sugar
1 egg
few drops vanilla essence (optional)
150 g (5 oz) plain flour
½ teaspoon bicarbonate of soda
pinch of salt
125 g (4 oz) chocolate chips
50 g (2 oz) walnuts or pecans

Set the oven at gas mark 5 (190°C) 375°F.

Beat the butter with both sugars until pale and fluffy, then beat in the egg and the vanilla essence.

Sift the flour with the bicarbonate of soda and the salt and beat into the mixture.

Stir in the chocolate chips and the finely chopped nuts.

Place small spoonfuls of the mixture on to well greased or non-stick baking tins, leaving plenty of room for the cookies to spread.

Bake for 10–15 minutes, until the little heaps have spread into thick cookies and are just beginning to turn golden brown.

Lift off the baking sheets and leave to cool and harden on a wire cake rack.

COUNTRY CRUNCH BARS

These crunchy uncooked chocolate bars are child's play to make, and everyone's pleasure to eat.

> *50 g (2 oz) butter or margarine*
> *200 g (7 oz) plain chocolate*
> *3 tablespoons golden syrup*
> *225 g (8 oz) plain digestive or rich tea biscuits*
> *icing sugar*

50 Put butter, chocolate and golden syrup in a small heavy

saucepan and heat gently, stirring until all the ingredients have melted and are thoroughly blended.

Break the biscuits into quite small pieces and stir into the mixture.

Pour into a greased shallow tin, approximately 18 cm (7 in) square and refrigerate for several hours till set.

Turn out of the tin, cut into bars and dust each bar lightly with icing sugar.

CHOCOLATE LIGHTNING THINS

The 'lightning' refers to the speed with which these are made and eaten.

> *125 g (4 oz) butter or margarine*
> *125 g (4 oz) sugar*
> *2 eggs*
> *100 g (3½ oz) plain flour*
> *2 tablespoons cocoa powder*
> *50 g (2 oz) almonds*
> *1 teaspoon ground cinnamon*
> *1 tablespoon sugar*

Set the oven at gas mark 6 (200°C) 400°F.

Cream the butter or margarine with the sugar until light and fluffy. Beat in the eggs one by one, then beat in the flour and cocoa, sifted together.

Spread thinly on a buttered 34 × 24 cm (13 × 10 in) baking sheet, or on several smaller ones – the mixture should not be more than ½ cm (¼ in) thick. Flake the almonds or chop them fairly finely, and scatter evenly over the top.

Blend the cinnamon into the sugar and sprinkle on evenly.

Bake for 20 minutes near the top of the oven, so that the almonds become lightly browned. Remove from the oven, leave to cool for a few minutes only, then cut into small squares or lozenge shapes and leave on a wire tray to cool. They will become quite crisp when cold, and should preferably be eaten on the day of making.

FLORENTINES

These are a little bit tricky to make at first, but so delicious that it is worth mastering the technique. Once you have done so, you will find them quite quick and simple to make. Store in airtight tins.

> *225 g (8 oz) almonds*
> *175 g (6 oz) mixed candied peel*
> *50 g (2 oz) glacé cherries*
> *50 g (2 oz) butter*
> *175 g (6 oz) caster sugar*
> *25 g (1 oz) plain flour*
> *300 ml (½ pint) double cream*
> *225 g (8 oz) plain or bitter chocolate*

Set the oven at gas mark 5 (190°C) 375°F.

Blanch the almonds and chop them. They may be chopped unevenly, so that some are fine and others are left quite chunky.

Chop the candied peel and the glacé cherries fairly finely.

Melt the butter and sugar together in a heavy saucepan over a moderate heat, stirring constantly and on no account allowing it to brown. When the mixture is fairly liquid (the sugar will not melt completely at this temperature) add the flour and continue to stir over a gentle heat until the mixture is quite smooth and comes away clean from the sides of the pan. Watch carefully that it does not brown.

Slowly add the cream, stirring well to keep the mixture smooth, then remove from the heat and add the almonds and fruit. Stir well.

Drop teaspoonfuls of the mixture on to buttered and floured or non-stick baking tins, leaving plenty of space between.

Place near the top of the oven and cook for 10–12 minutes, until they have spread and are lightly browned at the edges. Remove from the oven. At this point the florentines are still very malleable. If they have spread out too much and so will break too easily, or if indeed they have become merged with one another, it is easy to manoeuvre them back into shape with the top of a palette knife.

Leave to cool for 3 minutes on the baking sheets, then remove to a wire tray and leave to cool.

Melt the chocolate (in a bowl over a pan of boiling water) and thickly coat the flat side of each florentine, and place it, chocolate side up, on a tray or work surface. When all the florentines have been coated, make wavy lines on the chocolate with a fork. Leave to cool and set.

QUICK TRUFFLES

Very light, and quick and easy to make. They are excellent coated in chocolate, but this is not essential.

Best eaten fresh, but may be stored in the refrigerator for up to two weeks.

125 g (4 oz) plain or bitter chocolate
125 g (4 oz) unsalted butter
125 g (4 oz) icing sugar
2 teaspoons instant coffee powder (optional)
2 teaspoons brandy, rum or liqueur (optional)

For coating

2 tablespoons cocoa powder or 125 g (4 oz) plain
  or bitter chocolate
1 teaspoon tasteless salad oil

Melt the chocolate (in a bowl over a pan of boiling water). Leave to cool.

Beat the butter with the sugar until pale and fluffy.

Beat in the chocolate and the coffee and any spirits or liqueur.

Refrigerate the mixture for at least half an hour until it hardens enough to be rolled into balls or small sausage shapes.

Either roll these in cocoa, or melt the chocolate with the oil (as above) and coat each truffle in chocolate. Leave on foil to set.

CHOCOLATE FUDGE

Through many years of family fudge-making, this is the recipe that has proved the most consistently popular and successful, as well as requiring only the simplest of ingredients. However, it must be very carefully timed if the consistency is to come right.

> *300 ml (½ pint) milk*
> *450 g (1 lb) sugar*
> *25 g (1 oz) cocoa powder*
> *25 g (1 oz) butter*
> *½ teaspoon vanilla essence*
> *125 g (4 oz) chopped nuts or raisins (optional)*

Heat the milk with the sugar in a wide, heavy saucepan and stir until the sugar has dissolved. Add the cocoa and butter and bring slowly to the boil, stirring continuously so that the mixture becomes quite smooth. Continue to stir and boil until a temperature of 116°C (240°F) is reached on a sugar thermometer, or until a small amount of the mixture dropped into a glass of cold water forms a soft ball and does not make the water cloudy. This may take as much as 10–15 minutes, and the last few minutes are crucial as unless the correct temperature has been reached the fudge will not set. If it is exceeded, it will turn into toffee.

As soon as it reaches the 'soft ball' stage, remove the saucepan from the heat, add the vanilla and continue to stir or beat with a wooden spoon. When the mixture begins to thicken, add any chopped nuts or raisins you wish to use. Continue to beat until the mixture loses its gloss and becomes really thick and silky. Pour immediately into a buttered tin and leave in a cool place to set.

Cut into squares when set.

MONTEZUMA

Don't be fooled by the high milk content – this is a very potent drink, the summer counterpart of chocolate grog. Serve at the end of a summer evening party.

600 ml (1 pint) milk
75 g (3 oz) plain or bitter chocolate

pinch of allspice
pinch of ginger
1 tablespoon honey
75 ml (⅛ pint) rum
liqueur glass of eau de vie de marc or brandy
grated rind of ½ lemon

Heat the milk gently together with the chocolate, spices and honey, and stir until the chocolate has melted and the mixture is smooth. Leave to cool.

Pour the milk into a blender glass or a cocktail shaker, add remaining ingredients and blend or shake well.

Refrigerate and blend or shake again before serving.

ISABEL ALLENDE · *Voices in My Ear*

NICHOLSON BAKER · *Playing Trombone*

LINDSEY BAREHAM · *The Little Book of Big Soups*

KAREN BLIXEN · *From the Ngong Hills*

DIRK BOGARDE · *Coming of Age*

ANTHONY BURGESS · *Childhood*

ANGELA CARTER · *Lizzie Borden*

CARLOS CASTANEDA · *The Sorcerer's Ring of Power*

ELIZABETH DAVID · *Peperonata and Other Italian Dishes*

RICHARD DAWKINS · *The Pocket Watchmaker*

GERALD DURRELL · *The Pageant of Fireflies*

RICHARD ELLMANN · *The Trial of Oscar Wilde*

EPICURUS · *Letter on Happiness*

MARIANNE FAITHFULL · *Year One*

KEITH FLOYD · *Hot and Spicy Floyd*

ALEXANDER FRATER · *Where the Dawn Comes Up Like Thunder*

ESTHER FREUD · *Meeting Bilal*

JOHN KENNETH GALBRAITH · *The Culture of Contentment*

ROB GRANT AND DOUG NAYLOR · *Scenes from the Dwarf*

ROBERT GRAVES · *The Gods of Olympus*

JANE GRIGSON · *Puddings*

SOPHIE GRIGSON · *From Sophie's Table*

KATHARINE HEPBURN · *Little Me*

SUSAN HILL · *The Badness Within Him*

ALAN HOLLINGHURST · *Adventures Underground*

BARRY HUMPHRIES · *Less is More Please*

HOWARD JACOBSON · *Expulsion from Paradise*

P. D. JAMES · *The Girl Who Loved Graveyards*

STEPHEN KING · *Umney's Last Case*

LAO TZU · *Tao Te Ching*

DAVID LEAVITT · *Chips Is Here*

READ MORE IN PENGUIN

For complete information about books available from Penguin and how to order them, please write to us at the appropriate address below. Please note that for copyright reasons the selection of books varies from country to country.

IN THE UNITED KINGDOM: Please write to *Dept. EP, Penguin Books Ltd, Bath Road, Harmondsworth, Middlesex UB7 ODA.*

IN THE UNITED STATES: Please write to *Consumer Sales, Penguin USA, P.O. Box 999, Dept. 17109, Bergenfield, New Jersey 07621-0120.* VISA and MasterCard holders call 1-800-253-6476 to order Penguin titles.

IN CANADA: Please write to *Penguin Books Canada Ltd, 10 Alcorn Avenue, Suite 300, Toronto, Ontario M4V 3B2.*

IN AUSTRALIA: Please write to *Penguin Books Australia Ltd, P.O. Box 257, Ringwood, Victoria 3134.*

IN NEW ZEALAND: Please write to *Penguin Books (NZ) Ltd, Private Bag 102902, North Shore Mail Centre, Auckland 10.*

IN INDIA: Please write to *Penguin Books India Pvt Ltd, 706 Eros Apartments, 56 Nehru Place, New Delhi 110 019.*

IN THE NETHERLANDS: Please write to *Penguin Books Netherlands bv, Postbus 3507, NL-1001 AH Amsterdam.*

IN GERMANY: Please write to *Penguin Books Deutschland GmbH, Metzlerstrasse 26, 60594 Frankfurt am Main.*

IN SPAIN: Please write to *Penguin Books S. A., Bravo Murillo 19, 1° B, 28015 Madrid.*

IN ITALY: Please write to *Penguin Italia s.r.l., Via Felice Casati 20, I-20124 Milano.*

IN FRANCE: Please write to *Penguin France S. A., 17 rue Lejeune, F-31000 Toulouse.*

IN JAPAN: Please write to *Penguin Books Japan, Ishikiribashi Building, 2-5-4, Suido, Bunkyo-ku, Tokyo 112.*

IN GREECE: Please write to *Penguin Hellas Ltd, Dimocritou 3, GR-106 71 Athens.*

IN SOUTH AFRICA: Please write to *Longman Penguin Southern Africa (Pty) Ltd, Private Bag X08, Bertsham 2013.*